www.finishinglinepress.com

A Day in the Woods

poems by

Mia Eriksson

Finishing Line Press
Georgetown, Kentucky

A Day in the Woods

ACKNOWLEDGMENTS

I would like to thank my fellow poets in Jane Gregory's workshop *Introduction
to the writing of verse,* held at UC Berkeley during the spring semester of 2014.
Special thanks to Jane for her encouragement and support, and for making that
room such an inspiring place, full of trust, knowledge, and creativity. I would also
like to thank, with all my heart, Louise Daoust, Jackie Ballard, and Maria Guzman
for helping me promote this book. And, of course, my warmest thanks to Isabella
Hylin, not only for making such a beautiful cover but for being the most wonderful
friend imaginable. Thanks also to Richard Long at *2 River View* for accepting a
poem from a previously unpublished poet.

Publisher: Leah Maines

Editor: Christen Kincaid

Cover Art: Isabella Hylin

Author Photo: Kristofer Leifland

Cover Design: Elizabeth Maines

Printed in the USA on acid-free paper.

Order online: www.finishinglinepress.com
            also available on amazon.com

Author inquiries and mail orders:
Finishing Line Press
P. O. Box 1626
Georgetown, Kentucky 40324
U. S. A.

Table of Contents

for K

Apocalypse

After the bomb everything slowed down and the spiders came out
of their hiding to pave the roads.

Things that should not turn to stone turned to stone.
By now things have started to erode and

the trees stand perfectly still.
Their leaves fall with great deliberation.
The dead have ceased to decay.

During the nights that it does not rain
I go to bathe in the stars' light.
I pull them down and cut them up
and store them in my backyard

where the boxes of my childhood
are cracking up.

My Shanty

Morning on the hill is cool! Even the dead
grass stems that start with the wind along
the crude board fence are less than harsh.

Up where the lake ends
the sky starts, held off
by a blackened glass framed
into a wall partly shaded
by a lingering rooftop. This
is perfection is this
perfection left
hanging mid-air.
The lake has offered
to consume me, I am tempted.
Unwarranted the house
has burned the yellow grass down
the green trees birdless
offer no respite.
I had to leave the water out
it is too still to be painted.

William Carlos Williams, "Morning", in *Selected Poems*, edited by Charles
Tomlison, New York: New Directions Publishing (1985)

Ekphrasis poem of Georgia O'Keeffe's *My Shanty*

Driving

After a while my father
asks if my mother
is really fit to care for
small animals he says
they have been walking the streets
all night drinking she has
confessed things she shouldn't

Once I ran away from school
I was seven or eight I ran
into the street across it a dog
barked and a man asked
if I was lost if I needed help the dog
barked so loud it was the loudest
bark I ever heard the man
was as big as a monster I ran
in the other direction he was
probably trying to help

What a silly thing
my father says
and turns the car
radio volume up

Heroine

The light bulb lights
and paints the moon
in dim colors. I was born
with an arm for a head
I can turn the moon on
and off. I can reach
inside a bee hive
without getting stung
and lick up every drop of honey
that slips away. Windows
are shattered
and used as weapons
there is nothing that I
can do about that.
I can tear down the man
who thinks too highly
of himself with my mouth.

Unica Zürn

Shall I once more be rock solid?
                  You the movement, you the pull
no?

The scars crawl out at night.
                  Bats beating
like bombs, beating
my poor skull to pieces
then peace. Then evening?

I see only morning.
I paint the horses in colorful poison.

It's a text thing
                  don't you get it
I wanted all of you
My destiny, ha! Fuck your refusal Fuck
your death

It's their salt
                  I'm all sugar, crystal skin
I should have fought for you   (should have let you kill me)

Your birdprey body
                  not even
the width of a wing Fuck
I should have protected you

Mirror poem of Ana Božičević, "Poe", *The Volta: They Will Sew the Blue Sail*,
September 2012

Swimming

I wrote a million poems this week
each one like a knife, dull
ceaselessly stabbing the same old spot.
When did the trees stop talking,
the winds, the spring flowers
showing off their wombs
to the sun? The dead voices,
the killers, the revolutionaries
in their unicorn coats? Swimming
is a universal practice. Drowning
reserved for the lucky few

A mini-crown of four love sonnets

Winter

This is where it all began
with your hand half way up my –––, and the sand
I have a knot in my thigh, ingrained with a grain.
I was being literal about picking your brain

with a spoon. You're full of scabs but when you're naked
you shine like a ballpoint, an android
and you taste like a bit tongue, a mouthful
of blood, when I think of you I think of

being ripped apart. I think the snow is everything,
the way it muffles the sound of cars,
turns the world into an orchestra when melting,
stabs every shameful eye with light as bright as stars.

I walked willingly ahead
it was summer then.

Spring

It was summer then
you had been drinking
since your brute first threw
a fatherly fist at your sister

Everybody's got a childhood trauma
Shit lingers not like bruises but like
broken arteries or cardiac dysrhythmia
The coke makes you older see if I

care I always liked your ragged temper
and that you were gonna die young

I still go to Toronto
just to feel your eyes

on my shoulder I have put it down
as something insignificant

Fall

Something insignificant
like a shoulder covered only
with thin white cotton
on an unbearably hot day

or something like a sign / or a saying / if i cant
starved for attention
some thing
no one

ever did / as if / it mattered.
I loved you the most. I knew you
were a damaged motherfucker.
I held your whole body down
and it was light as a feather.
You were like a baby deer in the snow.

Summer

you were like a baby deer
in the snow, my darling euphemism
my Doctor Enemy God and Lucifer
I wonder about those

who do not want to kill themselves
are their veins less prevalent
their knives less decadent or their
convictions not worth fighting for

I can't remember now
if you smiled or not if I
choked or not if it
rained all day / as it always did

back then / I bury my feet in the sand
this is where it all began

A day in the woods

We kill them in the woods, sun's humming
Simon has the knife; he's bleeding from the head
The deer so happy in the warmth of the heather
We kill them in the woods, such tingling joy

Hush

Say man I am lost
Say man lost I am
Say lost I am man
Say I am man lost

Sew body on parts of wood
Sew wood body on parts of
Sew parts of wood on body
Sew on parts of body wood

Stand still like stone lies on earth
Stand like earth on stone lies still
Stand stone like earth still lies on
Stand earth lies still like on stone

Build a monster and feed him to the gods

Untitled / Sounds

o

This is what dark sounds like :

              Breath
                     stuck in chords

          A fistful
          of lungs

              Something
              slow
              moving
              and safe

o

It can be dangerous to go outside :

Cranberries come
up the cracks

to sing
of the slaughter

The poor
paved over, they found
twenty bodies
by a bus stop
no bother
to bury the poor
properly

o

Ordering food :

Dead bird
Dead fish
Dead pig
Dead cow
Dead human

    This is what light sounds like

o

They must necessarily yield to the force of circumstances :

> The radio speaks of home
> then there's no home
> or another home
> being taken away

> The skulls must be removed
> swiftly
> so they don't upset
> or get stolen

Andrew Jackson, Fifth Annual Message, December 3, 1833

Among the trees

It's all swimming but I'm tired
and cannot stay in place in where
a place takes place in the lake I'm
desperate there are the trees
and you see them and they speak

I was a deer I watched
the grass being measured
and carved and sold and
cities being built I was a deer
I was skin and bone

'Memory wound' will cut through site of Norway's massacre

I don't know why but I
like to write about carving
things in or out like a teenage
razor like a becoming I see
dead bodies when I close my eyes
with names carved into a wall with
flesh carved out of their skin

Huffington Post, July 3, 2014

The benches in the courtroom are made of wood the
trees remember everything they were there when
the world was burning for the first time when
names were an abundance of letters were names
fire

There is no smell
like a cut up tree
like burning sap
like a cold ocean
if it starts to rain it
has gotten out of hand :

I used to love the water

Det första skottet gick in i huvudet på pojken som låg ytterst. / Sedan siktade han mot hennes bakhuvud. Det vågiga kastanjebruna håret lyste vått i regnet. Skottet gick rakt genom huvudet och in i hjärnan. Han sköt igen. Nu mot hjässan. Också den kulan gick genom hjärnan. Den fortsatte ned genom halsen mot bröstkorgen och stannade vid hjärtat. Blodet pumpade ut. Det rann ned längs den unga kroppen, droppade ner på stigen, fuktade barren och samlades i små gropar på marken. / Sekunder efter träffades pojken som höll om henne. Skottet gick genom bakhuvudet. Kulan splittrades när den träffade hud, väv, ben. Splittren träffade lillhjärnan och krossade hjärnstammen. / Hjärtat slutade slå. / Från huvudet sipprade det ut litet blod. / Blodet blandades med regnvattnet och rann ner i jorden.

Åsne Seierstad, *En av oss: En berättelse om Norge*, Stockholm: Albert Bonniers Förlag (2013)

Smile or similitude or silly
soldier and sew the seer
back on hir back on the floor
            Oh you must hate this!
All the moaners think it matters
like you matter like a matter
of flesh that smile and smile you
see you are just like me

then the forest folded like a sack of skin
into a muddy pile of splinters
no one ever heard such a sound
a sigh
a wreck of raging thoughts of death
when it's quiet it's so quiet
like an empty sack of skin

Inside the tree is hollow
carvings of eyes your eyes
about your eyes
in silence it seems
I lost you
i

and plead we did not do this

Sometimes trees cause death
we have all forced a nail
through a bit of wood

I wish people were all trees and I think
I could enjoy them then

Georgia O'Keeffe, quoted in Erin B. Coe, Bruce Robertson and
Gwendolyn Owens, *Modern Nature: Georgia O'Keeffe and Lake George,*
London: Thames & Hudson (2013)

Afterword

Most of the poems in this collection were written between the summer of 2013 and the summer of 2014, while I was doing research for my PhD thesis in Gender Studies about the right wing terrorist attack in Norway on 22 July 2011. On that Friday afternoon, Anders Behring Breivik set off a homemade bomb outside of the government headquarters in Oslo, killing eight people, and then preceded to Utøya Island where the Labor Party's youth organization was holding its annual summer camp. For a little over an hour he walked around the island with a gun and a rifle, killing sixty-nine people and wounding many more. He was arrested and sentenced to twenty-one years in prison, with the possibility of extending his sentence for as long as he is considered a threat to society. The attack was inspired by a racist, anti-Muslim, anti-feminist and nationalistic ideology. These poems are a gathering place for the emotional debris that piled up during my research, but they are also explorations of the violence that I encountered in my research material and of the effects that it had on me; how it slowly became a part of my body, my thoughts and my dreams.

Mia Eriksson has a Ph.D. in Gender Studies and is currently working as a senior lecturer at Linnaeus University in Sweden. Her dissertation *Berättelser om Breivik: Affektiva läsningar av våld och terrorism* [Stories about Breivik: Affective readings of violence and terrorism] was published by Makadam Förlag in 2016. She writes poetry in both Swedish and English and her poem "A mini-crown of four love sonnets" has previously been published in *2 River View 19.2* (Winter 2015). *A Day in the Woods* is her poetry book debut. She lives in Malmö, Sweden.